I can write
a book called

"If I could talk to animals"

Bobbie Kalman
Crabtree Publishing Company
www.crabtreebooks.com

Created by Bobbie Kalman

For Debra Wilson and her dog Lavender,
who talk to each other—they really do!

Author and Editor-in-Chief
Bobbie Kalman

Editors
Kathy Middleton
Crystal Sikkens

Photo research
Bobbie Kalman

Prepress technician
Katherine Berti

Design
Bobbie Kalman
Katherine Berti
Samantha Crabtree
(logo and cover)

Print and production coordinator
Katherine Berti

Illustrations
Margaret Amy Salter: page 11

Photographs
Corel: pages 22 (top), 25 (bottom left)
iStockphoto: pages 10 (top right), 29 (top left)
© Bobbie Kalman: back cover-bottom, page 5 (top, except background art)
Thinkstock: page 25 (bottom right)
All other images by Shutterstock

Library and Archives Canada Cataloguing in Publication

Kalman, Bobbie
   I can write a book called "If I could talk to animals" / Bobbie Kalman.

(I can write a book series)
Includes index.
Issued also in electronic format.
ISBN 978-0-7787-7994-0 (bound).--ISBN 978-0-7787-8003-8 (pbk.)

   1. Animals--Juvenile literature. 2. Interviewing--Juvenile literature.
3. English language--Composition and exercises--Juvenile literature.
4. Book design--Juvenile literature. I. Title. II. Series: Kalman, Bobbie
I can write a book.

QL49.K3335 2012   j590   C2012-905688-X

Library of Congress Cataloging-in-Publication Data

CIP available at Library of Congress

Crabtree Publishing Company

www.crabtreebooks.com   1-800-387-7650

Printed in Canada/102012/MA20120817

Published in Canada
Crabtree Publishing
616 Welland Ave.
St. Catharines, Ontario
L2M 5V6

Published in the United States
Crabtree Publishing
PMB 59051
350 Fifth Avenue, 59th Floor
New York, New York 10118

Published in the United Kingdom
Crabtree Publishing
Maritime House
Basin Road North, Hove
BN41 1WR

Published in Australia
Crabtree Publishing
3 Charles Street
Coburg North
VIC 3058

Table of contents

Do you talk to animals?   4

How do they communicate?   6

What are these pages?   8

What words will I need?   10

What is an interview?   12

Which questions?   14

How will I do my research?   16

Are you ready to write?   18

Which text styles?   20

What senses do they use?   22

Will you type or write?   24

How can I revise it?   26

How will I design it?   28

What is left to do?   30

Bobbie's books   31

Glossary and Index   32

Do you talk to animals?

In your school or public library, you will find different kinds of books. **Fiction** books are written from someone's imagination and are not true. **Nonfiction**, or **informational**, books can contain facts about animals, habitats, countries, history, and many other subjects. They can also be **biographies**, or true stories about real people. This book shows you how to write and **publish** a book about animals, using both true facts and a lot of imagination. If you could **interview** animals, or ask them questions, what would you ask? Animals cannot answer using words, but they can **communicate**, or show what they mean or want, in other ways. Many pets are able to communicate with the people they live with.

You probably talk to your pets and show them what you want them to do. How do your pets let you know what they want or need?

How is this dog telling you that it wants to go for a walk?

What sounds do cats make when they are happy? What do you think this kitten is asking you to do?

This boy is trying to teach his dog how to "speak." What are some sounds that dogs make that people understand? Pretend you are a dog and make these sounds. Can your classmates guess what you are communicating in dog language?

Bobbie's dolphin "talk"

I love dolphins! I became very interested in these amazing animals in Hawaii, where I spent several months writing books about them. I swam with wild dolphins and visited captive dolphins several times a week. I "talked" and played with them. They made happy sounds when I arrived and splashed me with their tails. They threw balls at me and waved. I think they liked me.

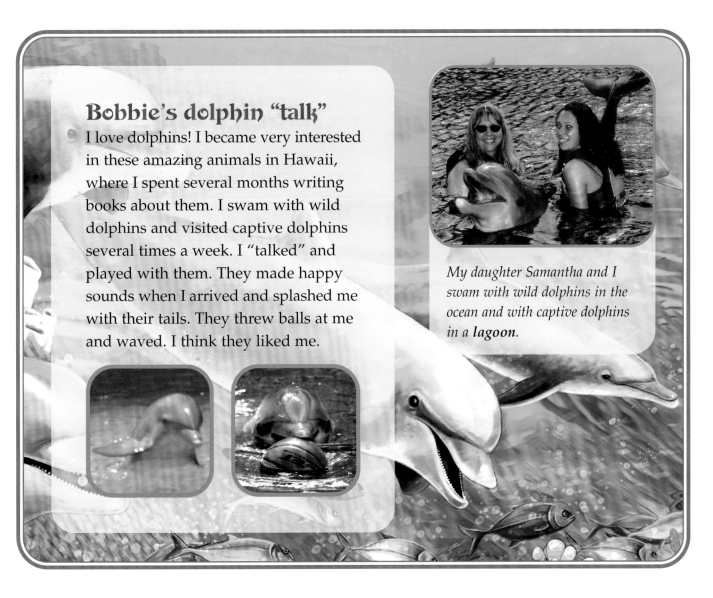

*My daughter Samantha and I swam with wild dolphins in the ocean and with captive dolphins in a **lagoon**.*

*Being an **author**, I need to learn a lot about the subjects of my books. When you write and publish a book, you will need to do the same. To publish is to share the final copy of your work with others.*

When you write your book, you will be "speaking" for the animals you have studied. Not only will you be an author, you will be a teacher, too, because your readers will learn about animals from you!

How do they communicate

People communicate information and feelings using words and **body language**. Body language includes facial expressions, such as smiles and frowns, and gestures made with hands and other body parts. Animals cannot speak, but they do make sounds and use body language to communicate, too. They also use their **senses** of sight, smell, taste, hearing, and touch to send and receive messages. How are the animals shown here communicating? Which senses are they using? Which animals are using body language?

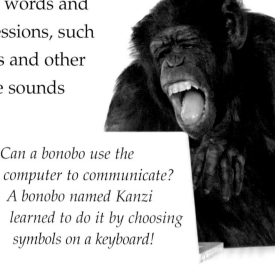

Can a bonobo use the computer to communicate? A bonobo named Kanzi learned to do it by choosing symbols on a keyboard!

This tiger cub cannot yet roar loudly enough to scare away his enemies. What does the body language of the cub say? Look at his ears. Is he happy or afraid?

*Anoles use their colorful throat sacs to attract mates or to make themselves look scarier to **predators**. Predators hunt and eat other animals.*

*Skunks use a strong **scent**, or smell, to make other animals, and people, stay away.*

hedgehog

*Hedgehogs and porcupines keep their predators away with their sharp spines. Porcupines can leave their spines stuck in a predator's skin. The spines have **barbs**, or hooks, at the ends that are very hard to remove.*

porcupine   spines

Some male birds, like the peacock above, **display**, or show off, their beautiful feathers to attract female birds. Other male birds sing, dance, or build nests to attract mates.

Elephants communicate with their **herd**, or family group, using **trumpet calls**, which they make by blowing air through their trunks. They can also hear **infrasound**, or low rumbling sounds, made by other elephants far away. Infrasound cannot be heard by humans.

This crane is dancing to attract a mate.

monarch butterfly

poison dart frog

The bright patterns on some butterflies and frogs let predators know that these animals taste awful or may even be poisonous.

This chimpanzee has learned to do **sign language**. Instead of using words, she uses body and hand movements to communicate. Do you think she is saying, "That's me" or "I'm hungry"?

Gray parrots and some other birds are able to learn to speak many words and even sing songs. People who teach them feel that the birds can understand the words they speak.

What are these pages?

Writing a book is like writing a report, but a book has more parts and pages. The pages are held together by a **cover**, or the protective outside page. It is the first part of a book that people see. The front cover tells you the book's title and the author's name. The back cover may give you information about the author, other books written by him or her, and the price of the book. The book's **spine** is what you see when the book is sitting on a shelf. It contains the book's title, author's name, and **publisher**. The publisher is the person or company that makes the book available to readers.

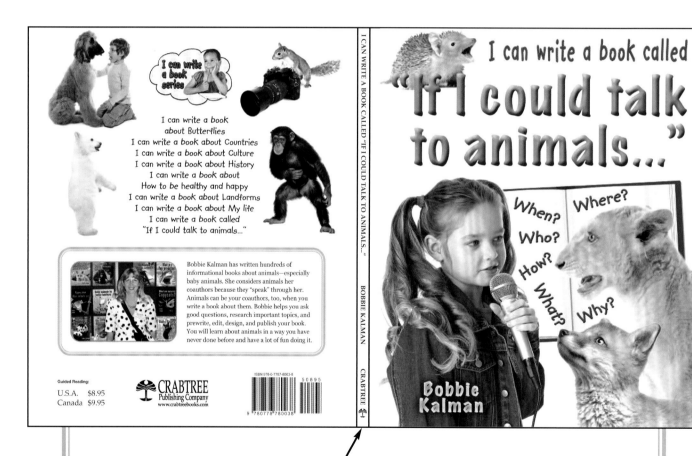

The back cover of the book may give you information about the author, publisher, price, and other books written by the author.

The spine of the book has the title, author, and publisher's name. It helps you find a book on a bookshelf.

The front cover of the book contains the title of the book and the name of the author. It catches your attention with an interesting title or a great picture or pictures.

The title page

The first page inside the cover is the **title page**. The picture on the right shows the title page of this book. What information does it give you?

Copyright page

The second page in this book is the **copyright** page. Copyright means that people cannot copy all or parts of the book without the author or publisher's permission. What else does it tell you? Turn to the copyright page in this book and find the following information:

- the names of the people who helped create this book
- the addresses of the publisher
- the **dedication** of the book, or the words used to honor someone by placing his or her name in the book
- the **cataloging information**, a section of the page that tells the books's title, the name of the author, the year the book was published, and the type of book it is

Contents, glossary, index

The **table of contents** is a list of the **chapters**, or sections, in the book and the page numbers on which they begin. The **glossary** is a small dictionary that explains special words used in the book. The **index** is an alphabetical list of the topics in the book with page numbers telling where those topics are covered.

The top picture shows the title page, and the bottom shows the table of contents of this book.

Table of contents

Do you talk to animals?	4	Which text styles?	20
How do they communicate?	6	What senses do they use?	22
What are these pages?	8	Will you type or write?	24
What words will I need?	10	How can I revise it?	26
What is an interview?	12	How will I design it?	28
Which questions?	14	What is left to do?	30
How will I do my research?	16	Bobbie's books	31
Are you ready to write?	18	Glossary and Index	32

What words will I need?

These two pages introduce some important words that you need to know about animals. The pictures and definitions give information that will help you write your book. For your own book, you can do a picture dictionary with definitions underneath, like the one on these pages, or a glossary without pictures, or both. (See pages 30 and 32 for how to write your glossary.)

An **amphibian** is an animal, such as a frog or toad, which starts its life in water and lives its adult life on land.

An **arthropod** is an animal without a backbone. Arthropods have legs that bend, and some have wings. Insects, spiders, and crabs are arthropods. These ants are arthropods, too.

A **carnivore** is an animal that eats mainly other animals. A predator hunts the animals it eats. **Prey** is an animal that a predator hunts.

An **endangered** animal is one that is in danger of dying out in the **wild**, or places not controlled by people. Many leopards are endangered.

Energy is the power **living things** (plants, animals, people) need to stay alive. All energy comes from sunlight.

Animals eat different kinds of food. A **food chain** is the passing of the sun's energy from one living thing to another through food.

Herbivores eat mainly plants. Carnivores eat other animals. **Omnivores** eat both plants and other animals.

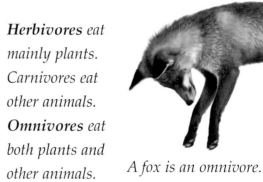

A fox is an omnivore. It eats plants and meat.

sunlight

sun's energy

plants

A rabbit is a herbivore.

A *forest* is a place in nature where many trees and other plants grow.

Grasslands are **habitats** with grasses and a few trees. A habitat is a place in nature where plants and animals live.

Hatching is breaking out of an egg. Birds, fish, and reptiles hatch from eggs.

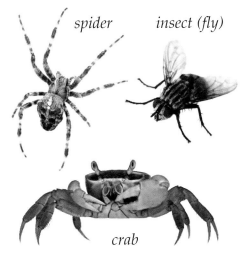

spider

insect (fly)

crab

An **invertebrate** is an animal that has no backbone. Insects, snails, spiders, worms, and crabs have no backbones.

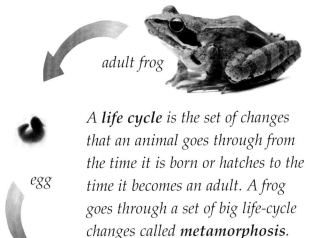

adult frog

egg

A **life cycle** is the set of changes that an animal goes through from the time it is born or hatches to the time it becomes an adult. A frog goes through a set of big life-cycle changes called **metamorphosis**.

froglet

tadpole

A **mammal** is an animal with a backbone and hair or fur. Mammal mothers **nurse**, or feed their babies milk from their bodies.

snake

A **reptile** is an animal with dry, scaly skin covering its body. Snakes, alligators and crocodiles, and turtles, are some reptiles. Most reptiles hatch from eggs. Reptiles are **vertebrates**, or animals with backbones.

turtle

backbone

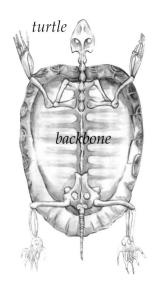

What is an interview?

In an interview, one person asks questions, and another person answers them. If you could interview an animal, what questions would you ask it? Animals cannot answer your questions using words, but don't let the questions go to waste! Use them as a guide to researching information. After you have done your research, you and your classmates could take turns interviewing one another. You could pretend to be the animals you have learned about and answer the questions as if you were those animals. Use the words below to begin your questions.

What? When? Why?

Where? Who?

Which? How?

red fox

When are you active and
when do you sleep?

leopards

Why are you endangered?
Who are your main enemies?

rabbit

Which animals
are your predators?
How do you hide
from them?

bobcat

Where is your habitat?
Is it in water or
on land?

What kind
of animal are you
pretending to be?

13

Which questions?

Before you start your research, read the questions below to help you decide what the subject of your book will be. Perhaps your teacher has asked you to do a report on a certain animal that you are studying. As shown on pages 12 and 13, many questions begin with the words what, where, when, who, why, which, and how. The best questions are those that require explanations and obtain good information about a subject. Weak questions can be answered with a "yes" or "no" or other one-word answer.

What is the habitat of these coyote pups?
Where is their home in this habitat?

Where do I start?
- Which animal do I want to research and why?
- What kind of animal is it?
- Where does it live?
- Why is it an important part of its habitat?
- How does it find food?
- What foods does it eat?
- Who are its enemies?
- What **defenses** does this animal use to survive? A defense is a way of stopping an attack from a predator.
- When is the animal awake and when does it sleep?
- What are the stages in the life cycle of this animal?

How do we make it fun?

You and your friends can practice creating good questions by interviewing one another. For fun, you could wear animal masks or paint your faces to look like the animals you are researching. Take photographs to use in your book.

Could I interview you?

When writing an interview, use **quotation marks** to show when one speaker stops and another begins. Quotation marks also show that you have used a speaker's exact words.

Q: "What type of animal are you?"

A: "I am a tiger, the biggest member of the cat family. Cats are mammals."

Q: "Where do you live?"

A: "I live in forests and grasslands near rivers or lakes. I like water."

Q: "What kind of food do you eat, and how do you find your food?"

A: "I am a carnivore and predator. I hunt deer, antelope, and wild pigs."

Q: "Why are you endangered?"

A: "I am losing my habitat because the forests where I live are being cut down. People also hunt me for my fur coat and other body parts. There are very few of us tigers left."

How will I do my research

Write down your interview questions and use them to start your research. Once you have chosen the animal you will write about, learn everything you can about that animal. The books on page 31 provide you with information on many subjects. You can also find information in other books, encyclopedias, **documentaries**, and on the Internet. Use at least two sources for your research. Read and understand the information and then rewrite it in your own words. You can also learn a lot about animals by **observing**, or watching them. When people observe animals and write books or make films about them, they are "speaking" for those animals. How will you be the voice of the animals you are researching?

Watching videos on the Internet is almost as good as watching them live! This bonobo is watching a video of himself in his jungle habitat in Africa. What emotions does his face show?

Working with other students will make your book more fun to research and write. You can each research a different animal and then interview one another to practice your question-and-answer skills.

If you have a pet, observe how it behaves and take some photographs of it. Write down the different sounds it makes, how it moves, and how it "talks" to you.

Research review

- Use at least two research sources.
- Write information in your own words.
- Observe an animal and write about what you have learned from watching it.
- Based on your observations, write a story about a day in the life of your animal.

monarch butterflies

elephant

ants

Go out in nature and make notes about the animals you see. What kinds of insects live in the grass? Which ones have wings and can fly?

Visit a zoo and observe the body language of some animals. Find out which ones are endangered and learn how you can help them.

giant panda and cub

Are you ready to write?

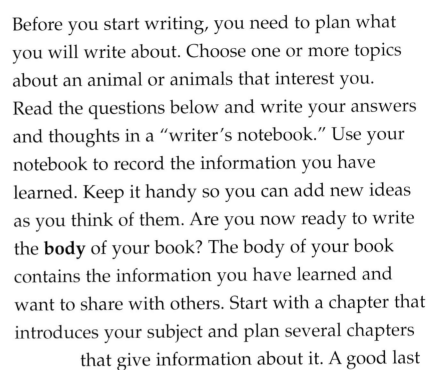

Before you start writing, you need to plan what you will write about. Choose one or more topics about an animal or animals that interest you. Read the questions below and write your answers and thoughts in a "writer's notebook." Use your notebook to record the information you have learned. Keep it handy so you can add new ideas as you think of them. Are you now ready to write the **body** of your book? The body of your book contains the information you have learned and want to share with others. Start with a chapter that introduces your subject and plan several chapters that give information about it. A good last chapter makes an important statement or challenges the reader with an activity.

What do I ask myself?

- Do I want to write about one animal or different kinds of animals?
- Which part of an animal's life do I want to learn more about?
- Why do I want to write about the topic I have chosen?
- Would my readers enjoy a book about the animal's life as a baby?
- In what ways does my animal communicate?

What is an outline?

Make an **outline** of the chapter headings that you will write about. Your outline will become your table of contents. Write your own chapter headings based on topics from these sample outlines. The outlines shown are written as questions. Write your outlines as questions, too. Questions will help you explore your topics.

What kind of animal is it?

What kinds of animals are there?

How do they grow and change?

What is an arthropod?

What is a reptile?

Which animals are amphibians?

What is a fish?

Can all birds fly?

What are mammals?

What is a life cycle?

How does the animal start its life?

Is it born, or does it hatch from an egg?

Does it hatch in water or on land?

What is its habitat as an adult?

How does the animal grow and change?

Does it go through metamorphosis?

Does its mother care for it as a baby?

How does she feed it?

When does the animal become an adult?

Where does it live?

What is the animal's habitat?

What is the climate where it lives?

How is the animal suited to its habitat?

Does the animal build a home?

How does it find food?

What role does it play in a food chain?

Is it an endangered animal?

What dangers does it face in its
   habitat today?

Which text styles?

Now that you have decided what you will write about, how will you write it? Informational writing gives facts, but your book could also contain other text styles, such as **narrative**, **descriptive**, and **rhyme** or **rap**. These text styles are shown on pages 20 to 23. On this page is an example of rhyming text called rap.

How will you rap about it?

Writing rap is a fun way to share information with your readers and help them remember it. They will want to read it out loud, listen to it, feel it, and move their bodies to the beat. Finding the right rhymes and beat can be challenging, so you may want to write your book with the help of some friends. Use the examples on this page to get you started.

I am an ape
called a chimpanzee.
I dance on two legs,
as you can see.
I move and dance
when I get the chance.

We foxes are omnivores
that eat plants and meat.
We are not fussy
about the foods we eat.
We eat mice and rabbits,
but we eat fruit, too.
For us omnivores,
any food will do.

We alligators and crocodiles
are animals called reptiles.
We swim in water and run on land
and love to sunbathe on the sand.

crocodile

alligator

"Will you tell our stories?"

Narrative text is written in story form. If animals could talk, they would have exciting stories to tell. Since they cannot talk, however, you can tell their stories for them. When baby animals are born or hatch, they face many dangers. After doing some research, write narratives for the babies on this page. These could be used as part of a book on life cycles.

1. Baby sea turtles hatch from eggs buried in sand on beaches. When the babies hatch, they dig out of the sand and crawl across the beach to their ocean home. Write about their dangerous journey and how the females come back to the same beach to lay eggs as adults.

2. Prairie dog pups are born in tunnels deep under the ground. Write about what the pups need to learn when they come above ground.

3. Baby crocodiles call out from their eggs to let one another know that it is time to hatch. By calling out and hatching together, their mother is more likely to hear them.

"Will I make it to the ocean before a predator catches and eats me?"

"How will we learn to survive?"

"Will our mother hear us and come back to the nest to protect us from predators?"

What senses do they use?

Descriptive text uses the five senses of sight, hearing, smell, taste, and touch to describe a place or thing. The stories on these two pages use descriptive text to describe the adventures of black bear cubs in their habitat. Look for the words in the stories that identify the senses the bears use while discovering their forest home. Use these "sense" words to write descriptive text about the daily adventures of the animal or animals in your book.

*"I am learning how to climb a tree in my forest home. As I climb, my body **touches** the bark. Can you guess how the bark **feels**?"*

*Which words on the right do you think describe the bark's **texture**, or how it **looks** and feels? Which words describe the opposite of the texture? If you do not know some of the words, look them up in a dictionary.*

bumpy
smooth
shiny
scratchy
flat
even
rough
velvety
uneven
rutted
itchy

"One day, while my mother and I were walking in a meadow, I **saw** a big male bear running toward us. I know that male bears like to eat cubs like me, so I jumped into a bush to hide. To scare the bear away, my mother made some loud noises." To listen to sounds made by mother and baby bears, go to this website: www.bear.org/website/bear-pages/black-bear/communication/29-vocalizations-a-body-language.html

"My mother warned me about skunks. She said if I go near one, I'll be sorry! When I did meet a skunk, I could hardly breathe. It really reeked!" Which words below describe a skunk's **smell**? Which words describe the opposite of the smell?

fragrant pungent foul putrid sweet
reeking aromatic sharp pleasant
disgusting strong bad stinky

"Like foxes, we bears are omnivores that eat plants as well as other animals. Today, I found some flowers to eat. They **tasted** sweet, but not as sweet as honey. I love honey so much that when I find a beehive, I eat the bees, too, even though they sting me. Ouch! Bee stings **hurt**!"

Will you type or write?

If you are writing your book on a computer, there are many **fonts** from which to choose.

- A font is a style of type. Most of this book is written in a **plain text** font, but you will notice other kinds of fonts, as well.
- Some words on pages 22 and 23 are in a **boldface**, or thick black font, to bring attention to a subject. Other boldfaced words may be new to you. They are explained where they appear in the book or are defined in the glossary at the end of the book.
- **Headings** tell you what chapters are about. **Subheadings** tell you what paragraphs are about. A different font and size can be used to make them stand out from the rest of the text.
- **Fact boxes** give instructions, bring attention to special information, or ask questions. The fact boxes in this book are on notebook pages, like the one shown here on the right.

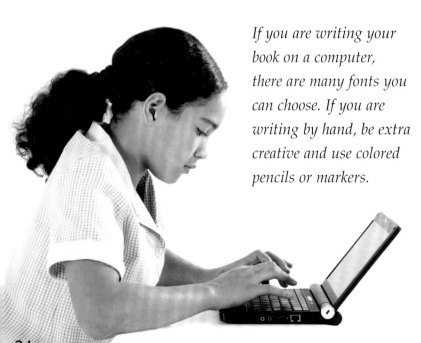

If you are writing your book on a computer, there are many fonts you can choose. If you are writing by hand, be extra creative and use colored pencils or markers.

Fonts and writing

- If you are using a computer, try different fonts.
- Choose a plain text font that is easy to read.
- Choose heading fonts that suit your subject.

Chapter headings are in large colored type.

Subheadings are smaller than chapter headings and may also be in color.

- If you are writing your book by hand, use a thick pencil, pen, or marker to make words look **boldfaced**.
- Write **captions** by *slanting* your words to look like an *italic* font (see next page).
- For headings, use markers or colored pencils.

What are captions?

The text that gives information about a picture is called a caption. The captions in this book are written in a slanted font called *italics*. Words in italics slant to the right. A caption can give information, ask questions, or challenge you to use your imagination. Since this book is about talking to animals, you can be really creative with your captions.

Why are these animals laughing? Do they want to have their pictures taken by the squirrel photographer? Write a funny caption pretending to be each of these animals.

What is a photo essay?

If you have a lot of pictures, you may want to write part or all of your book as a **photo essay**. A photo essay gives information or tells a story using words and photos. A photo essay is usually written in plain text.

This cougar cub has wandered away from her home. If a wolf or grizzly bear finds her, she will be in trouble! Predators often hunt baby animals— even baby predators like cougars.

The cub is lucky! Her mother has found her and is taking her to a new home. Mother cougars move their cubs often so predators will not find them.

How can I revise it?

Once you have written your **draft**, or first try at writing your book, it is time to read it to yourself. While reading, ask yourself these questions:

- How does my writing sound?
- Have I included all the information I needed to include?
- Have I used different text styles to write my book?
- Do my captions give interesting information? Do they describe what is happening in the pictures?
- Do my sentences make sense?
- Do my questions make my readers think?
- How can I **revise**, or rewrite, my book to make it better?

Have I written about my own observations or experiences with animals?

How can I make my book sound better? What changes does it need?

Ask a parent or your teacher to look over your writing and make some suggestions about ways to revise your book.

What are editing and proofreading?

After you have read your draft and revised it, it is time to share it with others. Ask a parent, classmate, or older sibling to **edit** your work. To edit is to read, check facts, and rewrite parts of someone's writing.

• What questions did the editors ask?

• What did they not understand?

• What suggestions did they make?

After you have made the suggested changes, it is time to **proofread** your book. To proofread is to check for errors in spelling, **punctuation**, and use of **capital** letters to start names and sentences. Punctuation marks include periods, question marks, and commas. What other punctuation marks are there?

*A dictionary gives you the correct spelling and meaning of words. A **thesaurus** helps you find several **synonyms** for a word. A synonym is a word that means the same as another word. If you are writing on a computer, you can use an online dictionary and thesaurus.*

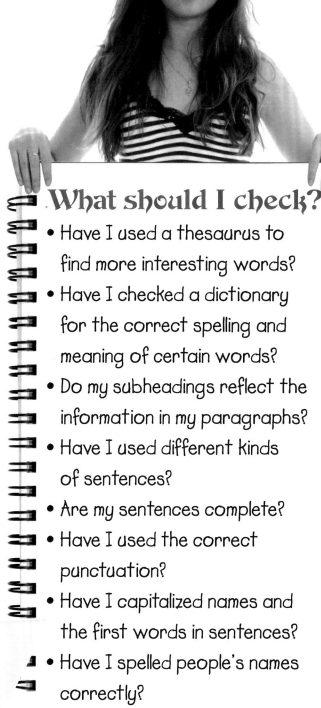

What should I check?

• Have I used a thesaurus to find more interesting words?

• Have I checked a dictionary for the correct spelling and meaning of certain words?

• Do my subheadings reflect the information in my paragraphs?

• Have I used different kinds of sentences?

• Are my sentences complete?

• Have I used the correct punctuation?

• Have I capitalized names and the first words in sentences?

• Have I spelled people's names correctly?

How will I design it?

Designing is planning how your book will look so that people will want to read it. Using fact boxes and photographs with captions is part of design. Different fonts and colors also make the book look more attractive to readers.

How can I make it look good?

Using exciting, cute, or funny pictures will make people want to read your book. You can create your own pictures of animals or download photos from the Internet. Ask a parent or teacher to help you find pictures that are free to use. Print these pictures and put them into your book. Look at the design of the pages in this book to give you more ideas about how to design your own book.

Use photographs that you have taken of your pet, a zoo animal, or an animal that lives in your yard or nearby park.

You can also draw and paint your own animal pictures. What is this chimpanzee painting for her book?

I can talk to animals!

About the author
Write something about yourself, how you wrote this book, and why people should read it.

I can talk to animals!   Author's name

Author's name

Above is an example of a front and back cover. You can draw pictures, use your own photos, or download some from the Internet. For your title page, draw a different picture or use your cover picture again.

To publish your book, photocopy all your handwritten pages and art. Save your original pages to make extra copies of your book if you need them. If you did your book on a computer, print off as many copies as you need or share your book online with your classmates.

How will I bind it?

An easy way to **bind**, or tie the pages of your book together, is to place them in binders with plastic page protectors, such as the ones shown below. Some binders have plastic pockets on the front and back, as well. You can slide your cover pictures into those. The thin plastic pocket on the spine will hold the book's title and your name.

What is left to do?

Before you publish your book, make sure you have completed all the pages shown here. These pages are very important because they help readers find and understand information in your book and credit the people who helped you. You can also include a **bibliography**. A bibliography is a list of books and authors that you used for your research, as well as the sources of your photographs and art.

Copyright page

Your copyright page will include the names of all the people who helped you with your book: other writers, editors, proofreaders, photographers, and artists. This page may also include a dedication. To whom will you dedicate your book?

Glossary

Make a picture dictionary or word glossary and put it at the end of your book. Define special words that your readers may not know. Sort the words in alphabetical order.

Index

The index is a list of the topics in the book. It should also be in alphabetical order and give the page numbers of where the topics can be found (see the glossary and index on page 32).

Table of contents

Your table of contents is a list of the chapter headings in your book. The page numbers can be placed at the left or right of the headings (see page 3).

Bobbie's books

The books shown here were written by me, Bobbie Kalman, and my animal friends. These books will help you write your own book about animals. You can find them—and many more written by me—in your school or public library.

The books shown above are just a few of the many books I have written about animals. My series It's fun to learn about Baby Animals and The Habitats of Baby Animals were especially fun to write. The photographs are really cute and amazing! Perhaps you will write about baby animals, too.

Glossary

Note: Some boldfaced words are defined where they appear in the book.

biography A true story about someone's life written by another person

communicate To pass along information through sounds and signs

descriptive text A writing style that uses the five senses of sight, hearing, smell, taste, and touch

documentary A movie or TV show about real people, events, or animals

informational text A writing style that gives information

infrasound Sound that cannot be heard by humans but can be felt as vibrations

invertebrate An animal without a backbone

lagoon A shallow area at the edge of an ocean, which is partly enclosed and sheltered by rocks or coral reefs

metamorphosis The total change of an animal's body from one form to another

narrative A writing style that tells something in story form

punctuation The use of marks, such as periods or commas, to make the meaning of a sentence clear

sign language A way of communicating using hand gestures

vertebrate An animal with a backbone

Index

body language 6, 17
caption 24, 25, 26, 28
communication 4, 6, 7, 18
copyright 9, 30
cover 8, 9, 29
design 28–29
draft 26, 27
editing 27
endangered 10, 13, 15, 17, 19
fact boxes 24, 28

fonts 24, 25, 28
glossary 9, 10, 24, 30
habitats 11, 13, 14, 15, 16, 19, 22
headings 24, 27, 30
index 9, 30
interview 4, 12, 15, 16
observing 16, 17
outlines 19
pictures 8, 9, 10, 15, 17, 25, 26, 28, 29

predators 6, 7, 13, 14, 15, 21, 25
proofreading 27
questions 4, 12, 14–15, 16, 18, 19, 24, 25, 26
research 12, 14, 15, 16–17, 21, 30
revising 26, 27
sounds 4, 5, 6, 17, 23
table of contents 9, 19, 30
text styles 20–23, 26